What Do I Do with My Money?

written by
Hady A. Hamid

art by
Muhammad Ali

of

SUNSETRAIN
creatives

To order additional copies of this book, contact
Toll Free +65 3165 7531 (Singapore)
Toll Free +60 3 3099 4412 (Malaysia)
www.partridgepublishing.com/singapore
orders.singapore@partridgepublishing.com

ISBN
ISBN: 978-1-5437-6354-6 (sc)
ISBN: 978-1-5437-6356-0 (hc)

Print information available on the last page.

02/15/2021

PARTRIDGE

Dedication

*"To my wife, who taught me how to budget.
To my son, whom I'm counting down
the days before you lose your babyhood.
And to my daughter, whom I pass on
my budgeting techniques and my love.*

*And to all the parents and parents-to-be whom
I hope can and will benefit from this book.
All the best!"*

BunBun
A mild-mannered bunny who always wants the best
for his family, BunBun has recently adopted a more hands-on
and thorough approach towards his family finances
to better navigate through life's uncertainties.

Kitty
A former senior manager at a reputable company,
the now-homemaker Kitty does her best to manage
the household matters, especially ones that involve
her two cute children, whom she cares for very much.

Redhead
The elder and more outgoing of the two children,
Redhead is a highly-curious and introspective kitten,
always wondering to herself about the best ways
she could carry out her tasks and duties.

Stoneface
The younger and more reserved child, Stoneface is
the little bundle of joy that everyone babies
because he's basically still…a baby bunny.
He's just there.

When I was little, I only knew a few things.
To always say, "Please", "Thank you" and "Sorry".
But when I started school, I needed to think,
About another thing that filled me with worry.

On my first day, Papa gave me two dollars.
He said, "Be a good girl, and spend it wisely."
As he kissed my forehead, and fixed my collar,
I wondered to myself, "How can I do this nicely?"

I looked at how my friends spent their money.
They bought a lot of things, and they didn't care.
But Papa worked hard for us, he's a caring bunny.
To disappoint him so much, I wouldn't dare.

When I got home, I went to Mama for advice.
I asked her, "What do I do with my money?"
She knelt down with a warm smile so nice,
"I'm glad you asked. Let me show you, honey."

One day, Mama brought me to the supermarket.
There were so many things that caught my eye.
But Mama only put a few things in the basket.
She said, "Take only the things we need to buy."

I asked Mama, "What do we need at home?"
She answered, "Only groceries and cleaning supplies."
With this in mind, my eyes started to roam,
And saw many things I didn't need, to my surprise

When we came home, Mama smiled and said to me,
"Look at how much I still have, honey."
She had fifty dollars, and came back with twenty.
Now I know what to do with my money!

Next day, I only spent what I needed at school.
I bought just one dish, and then drank plain water.
I was so happy I was able to do something cool,
I couldn't wait to tell Mama I was a good daughter!

I came home, and shouted, "Mama! Mama! I did it!"
I hugged her, and said, "I only spent what I needed!"
Mama hugged me tighter, and said, as her eyes lit,
"I'm so proud of you, Redhead! You've succeeded!"

Later, Mama told Papa what happened that day.
I was happy Papa knew that I smiled so widely.
Papa high-fived me, and said, "You did okay..."
"...so this is what you get when you spend wisely."

Papa took out a box, and asked for my spare change.
He put my change into the box, and then he put his.
Papa looked at me, and said, "This is what I've arranged..."
"...for you to grow your money properly with this."

Papa said, "With every cent you save, I'll match it..."
"...so I hope you'll continue this daily routine."
Feeling so happy, I hugged Papa tightly for a bit,
For teaching me early what spending wisely means.

OUR THANKS

I hope you enjoyed the story, and learned the valuable lesson about how you should spend your money.

Being able to manage your money is a good skill to learn while you are still young, so that you can be really good at it when you grow up, and have more money with you!

~ ~ ~ ~ ~ ~ ~ ~ ~ ~ ~ ~ ~ ~ ~ ~ ~ ~ ~

So now that you've seen how I manage my money, why don't you try it out!

Get your mommy and daddy to help you out so you can try and learn how to manage your money for three months first.

Afterwards, if you still want to continue, ask your parents to download more of the budget tracker by following the Instagram account: sunsetrain.creatives

EXAMPLE	ALLOWANCE	EXPENSES	NET BALANCE	MATCHING AMOUNT	TOTAL AMOUNT
MON	$2	$1 *minus*	$1 *equals*	*from parents* $1 *plus*	$2 *equals*
TUE	$2	$2	$0	$0	$0
WED	$2	$1.50	$0.50	$0.50	$1
THU	$2	$0.50	$1.50	$1.50	$3
FRI	$2	$1.90	$0.10	$0.10	$0.20
SAT	$2	$0.70	$1.30	$1.30	$2.60
SUN	$2	$0	$2	$2	$4

WEEKLY GRAND TOTAL $12.80

affix sticker here

WEEK 01	ALLOWANCE	EXPENSES	NET BALANCE	MATCHING AMOUNT	TOTAL AMOUNT
MON					
TUE					
WED					
THU					
FRI					
SAT					
SUN					

WEEKLY GRAND TOTAL

paste sticker here

WEEK 02	ALLOWANCE	EXPENSES	NET BALANCE	MATCHING AMOUNT	TOTAL AMOUNT
MON					
TUE					
WED					
THU					
FRI					
SAT					
SUN					

WEEKLY GRAND TOTAL

paste sticker here

WEEK 03	ALLOWANCE	EXPENSES	NET BALANCE	MATCHING AMOUNT	TOTAL AMOUNT
MON					
TUE					
WED					
THU					
FRI					
SAT					
SUN					

WEEKLY GRAND TOTAL

paste sticker here

WEEK 04	ALLOWANCE	EXPENSES	NET BALANCE	MATCHING AMOUNT	TOTAL AMOUNT
MON					
TUE					
WED					
THU					
FRI					
SAT					
SUN					

WEEKLY GRAND TOTAL

paste sticker here

WEEK 05	ALLOWANCE	EXPENSES	NET BALANCE	MATCHING AMOUNT	TOTAL AMOUNT
MON					
TUE					
WED					
THU					
FRI					
SAT					
SUN					

WEEKLY GRAND TOTAL

paste sticker here

WEEK 06	ALLOWANCE	EXPENSES	NET BALANCE	MATCHING AMOUNT	TOTAL AMOUNT
MON					
TUE					
WED					
THU					
FRI					
SAT					
SUN					

WEEKLY GRAND TOTAL

paste sticker here

WEEK 07	ALLOWANCE	EXPENSES	NET BALANCE	MATCHING AMOUNT	TOTAL AMOUNT
MON					
TUE					
WED					
THU					
FRI					
SAT					
SUN					

WEEKLY GRAND TOTAL

paste sticker here

WEEK 08	ALLOWANCE	EXPENSES	NET BALANCE	MATCHING AMOUNT	TOTAL AMOUNT
MON					
TUE					
WED					
THU					
FRI					
SAT					
SUN					

WEEKLY GRAND TOTAL

paste sticker here

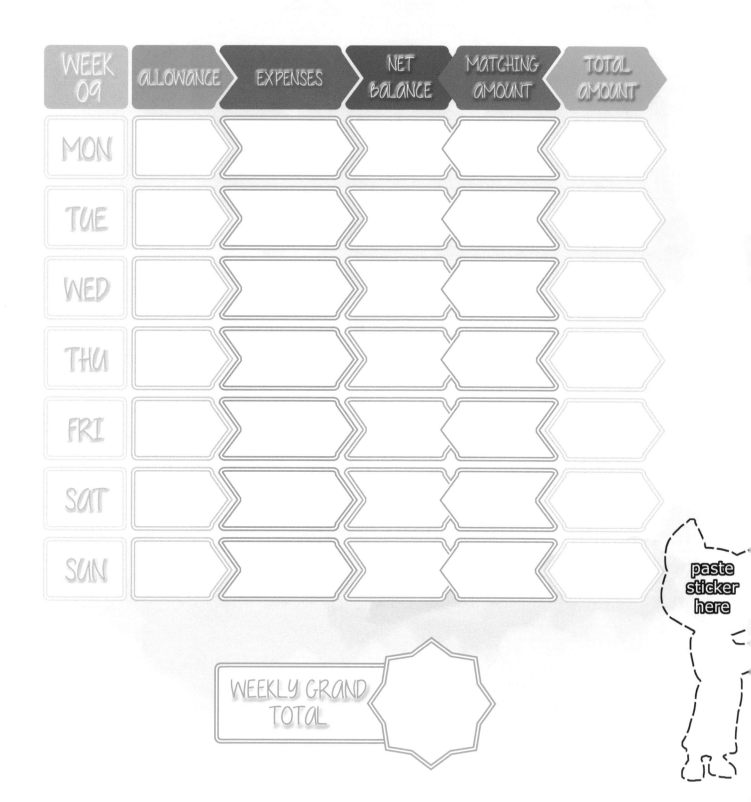

WEEK 09	ALLOWANCE	EXPENSES	NET BALANCE	MATCHING AMOUNT	TOTAL AMOUNT
MON					
TUE					
WED					
THU					
FRI					
SAT					
SUN					

WEEKLY GRAND TOTAL

paste sticker here

WEEK 10	ALLOWANCE	EXPENSES	NET BALANCE	MATCHING AMOUNT	TOTAL AMOUNT
MON					
TUE					
WED					
THU					
FRI					
SAT					
SUN					

WEEKLY GRAND TOTAL

paste sticker here

WEEK 11	ALLOWANCE	EXPENSES	NET BALANCE	MATCHING AMOUNT	TOTAL AMOUNT
MON					
TUE					
WED					
THU					
FRI					
SAT					
SUN					

WEEKLY GRAND TOTAL

paste sticker here

WEEK 12	ALLOWANCE	EXPENSES	NET BALANCE	MATCHING AMOUNT	TOTAL AMOUNT
MON					
TUE					
WED					
THU					
FRI					
SAT					
SUN					

WEEKLY GRAND TOTAL

paste sticker here

About the Author

A senior financial services consultant from MFA Group, Hady has amassed a clientele of at least 300 individuals, ranging from mass market to the affluent, and even corporate entities. He constantly upgrades himself, and most recently, has been successfully certified in Business Insurance Planning by the Singapore College of Insurance, and in Islamic Banking and Takaful by the Chartered Institute of Management Accountants.

Hady has spoken at several seminars and workshops from 2018 to 2020. He mostly covers topics such as family financial planning and financial fundamentals for Muslims. Most recently, as part of his endeavor to promote the importance of business insurance for Muslim business owners, he spoke at a seminar for business owners organised by the Singapore Malay Chamber of Commerce and Industries.

As a family man, Hady has been inculcating in his two children an attitude of financial awareness and discipline, and since the majority of his clients also have children, he wants to share some of his ideas with them.

About the Artist

An artist through-and-through, Ali constantly updates himself with new methods and techniques in character design, lighting and colouring in order to produce better quality throughout the years. With a Diploma in Digital Media Design from Nanyang Polytechnic, he has completed several commissioned artworks as well, serving clients such as Monochromatic Pictures, Flip! Creatives, Singapore Police Force and National Library Board.

Ali is the co-founder and artist of Sacred Comics, a self-funded comic book label that he has been developing with Hady since 1996. The project explores super-powered characters rooted in Islamic traditions and lore.

Ali has recently taken an interest in game design as part of his new personal project, Terra Obxcura, which he updates on his Instagram account @0bxcura

Lightning Source UK Ltd.
Milton Keynes UK
UKHW051447240221
379289UK00002B/5

9 781543 763560